Long-Term Forest Health Monitoring Program in the Eastern Mountains and Rivers Network

Evaluation of the Statistical Power to Detect Temporal Trends

Natural Resource Technical Report NPS/ERMN/NRTR—2012/637

Stephanie J. Perles[1], Tyler Wagner[2], Brian Irwin[3], Douglas R. Manning[1], Kristina K. Callahan[1], and Matthew R. Marshall[1]

[1]National Park Service
Northeast Region
Eastern Rivers and Mountains Network
Forest Resources Building
University Park, Pennsylvania 16802

[2]United States Geologic Survey
Pennsylvania Cooperative Fish and Wildlife Research Unit
402 Forest Resources Building
University Park, Pennsylvania 16802

[3]United States Geologic Survey
Georgia Cooperative Fish and Wildlife Research Unit
Warnell School of Forestry and Natural Resources
University of Georgia
Athens, GA 30602

October 2012

U.S. Department of the Interior
National Park Service
Natural Resource Stewardship and Science
Fort Collins, Colorado

The National Park Service, Natural Resource Stewardship and Science office in Fort Collins, Colorado, publishes a range of reports that address natural resource topics of interest and applicability to a broad audience in the National Park Service and others in natural resource management, including scientists, conservation and environmental constituencies, and the public.

The Natural Resource Technical Report Series is used to disseminate results of scientific studies in the physical, biological, and social sciences for both the advancement of science and the achievement of the National Park Service mission. The series provides contributors with a forum for displaying comprehensive data that are often deleted from journals because of page limitations.

All manuscripts in the series receive the appropriate level of peer review to ensure that the information is scientifically credible, technically accurate, appropriately written for the intended audience, and designed and published in a professional manner.

Views, statements, findings, conclusions, recommendations, and data in this report do not necessarily reflect views and policies of the National Park Service, U.S. Department of the Interior. Mention of trade names or commercial products does not constitute endorsement or recommendation for use by the U.S. Government.

This report is available from the Eastern Rivers and Mountains Network website (http://science.nature.nps.gov/im/units/ERMN) and the Natural Resource Publications Management website (http://www.nature.nps.gov/publications/NRPM).

Please cite this publication as:

NPS 962/117418, October 2012

Contents

Figures

Tables

Acknowledgements

We thank park superintendents, resource managers, and staff who have provided valuable logistic support to field crews. We also thank forest monitoring field crew members Greg Short, Larry Klotz, Joseph Pekol, Derrick Etter, Tom Saladyga, John Wiley, Steven Murphy, and Paul Beaver, whose hard work collecting data made this research possible. We extend our thanks to Jim Comiskey, John Paul Schmit, Paul Roth, and Leigh Ann Starcevich for providing constructive feedback on this report, and to Emily Hill for formatting and editing assistance.

The use of trade names or products does not constitute endorsement by the U.S. Government.

Executive Summary

We evaluated the power of the ERMN Forest and Soil Monitoring Program's sampling design to detect trends in 30 key forest health variables. We used a simulation approach to examine the statistical power to detect temporal trends in 17 non-count variables and four count variables using the variance components estimated from mixed models. We were unable to perform power analyses for nine of the count variables because mixed models failed to converge (i.e., estimates of variance components were not achieved).

We investigated the extent to which the following factors affected the ability to detect a trend: a) using a simple panel versus a connected panel design; b) increasing the trend magnitude (λ ranging from a 1% to a 10% change in the forest metric·year^{-1}); c) varying sample size in relation to park size (ranging from 3–25 plots·year^{-1}); c) post-stratifying the plots into vegetation domains (xeric and mesic); and d) increasing the coherent temporal variation (from 0–10% of total variation)

The program's sampling design at the two largest network parks is likely overly intensive for detecting a 5% trend · year^{-1} for all the variables, is appropriate for detecting a 1% trend · year^{-1} in most variables, and is insufficient for detecting a 1% trend · year^{-1} for a few variables. However, these power estimates are "best case scenarios" since the estimates of coherent temporal variation and estimates of trend variation were likely underestimated based on only four to five years of data. If the true value of coherent temporal variation is larger than the values used in the simulations for many of the key variables, then actual power will be lower than reported here. Although the power curves reported are potentially overly-optimistic, they suggest that the current sampling design is meeting the program's objectives.

The total variance appeared more influential in determining power than the structure of the variance components. Variables that measure the proportion of a total (i.e., species richness or percent cover) yielded much higher power than variables that measure absolute or average values since using the proportion reduces the variability in measurements caused by yearly weather patterns and different observers.

There are sufficient samples in the four larger ERMN parks to post-stratify plots by vegetation domains and retain adequate power. In the smaller parks, the small sample sizes currently employed are sufficient to detect small trends (1%·year^{-1}) in some important variables (e.g., live tree basal area); however, for some variables (e.g., coarse woody debris volume), only larger trends (5% · year^{-1}) are able to be detected.

The connected panel design which was implemented during the first sampling cycle does not provide sufficient additional power over the simple panel design to justify the additional sampling cost. Moving forward, the ERMN will employ a simple panel design.

Introduction

In 2007, the Eastern Rivers and Mountains Network (ERMN) of the National Park Service (NPS) began monitoring vegetation communities and soil in eight of its nine parks. This monitoring effort is a component of the ERMN Vital Signs monitoring program (Marshall and Piekielek 2007) and part of the nationwide NPS Inventory and Monitoring Program (Fancy et al. 2009).

The ERMN includes nine parks in New York, New Jersey, Pennsylvania, and West Virginia (Figure 1) which together encompass nearly 91,000 ha of land area and over 965 km of streams and rivers within the parks' authorized boundaries. The network includes four smaller parks in central and southwestern Pennsylvania that have a primarily cultural or historical focus. The cultural parks are Allegheny Portage Railroad National Historic Site (ALPO), Johnstown Flood National Memorial (JOFL), Fort Necessity National Battlefield (FONE), and Friendship Hill National Historic Site (FRHI). The five larger parks preserve segments of large rivers and generally extend to the ridge tops surrounding the river section. The river parks are Upper Delaware Scenic and Recreational River (UPDE), Delaware Water Gap National Recreation Area (DEWA), New River Gorge National River (NERI), Gauley River National Recreation Area (GARI), and Bluestone National Scenic River (BLUE).

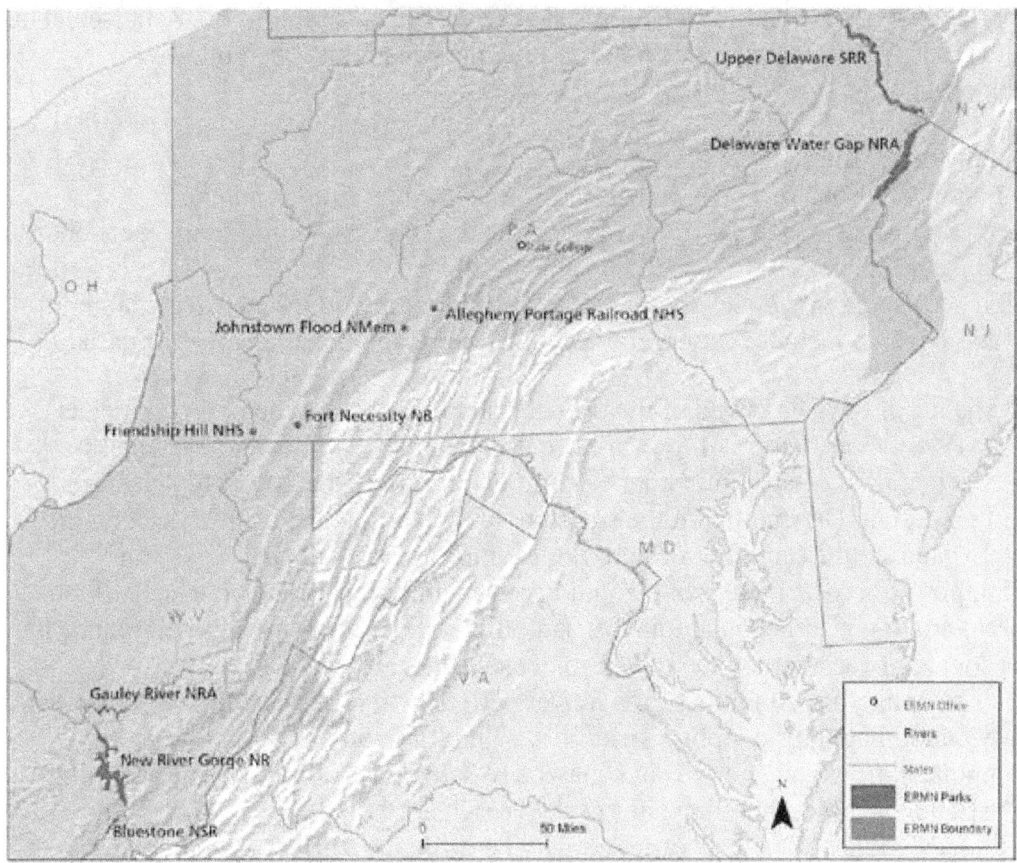

Figure 1. Locations of ERMN parks.

Long-term monitoring of vegetation and soils was identified among the highest priority vital signs during the ERMN prioritization process (Marshall and Piekielek 2007). The vital sign process highlighted the importance of plant species diversity and functional plant communities as natural resources critical to the parks. Vegetation communities also serve as an integrated measure of terrestrial ecosystem health by expressing information about climate, soils, and disturbance. Furthermore, vegetation serves as a base for other trophic components such as wildlife.

The ERMN Vegetation and Soil Monitoring Program provides information regarding the condition of these resources in the parks, and how this condition is changing through time. In order to be effective, the monitoring program must be able to detect changes in the parks' vegetation within a reasonable period of time, with a reasonable level of statistical confidence. Power analysis is a useful tool for evaluating the performance of ecological monitoring programs (Peterman 1990, Fairweather 1998, Hatch 2003), and, in particular, for investigating how specific variance components affect the power to detect trends for a given sampling design (Urquhart et al. 1998).

One approach to evaluating trends in forest vegetation is to use estimated structures of variance to evaluate the statistical power of different sampling designs. A components of variance approach has been advocated to address the issue of variability in ecological data when evaluating temporal trends and monitoring ecological systems (Urquhart et al. 1998, Larsen et al. 2001, Kincaid et al. 2004). Under this framework, total variance is partitioned into five components, including:

1. spatial variation (site-to-site);
2. coherent temporal variation (year-to-year) affecting all sites in a similar manner;
3. ephemeral temporal variation (i.e., a site x year interaction) corresponding to independent yearly variation at each site;
4. trend variation corresponding to site-specific deviations from any long-term average trend;
5. residual variation, which includes observer error and other unexplained sources of variation.

Although total variance of the data is one of the primary factors affecting the ability to detect trends (Stow et al. 1998), the structure of the variance is also important. Power analysis is a useful tool for investigating how specific variance components affect the power to detect trends for a given sampling design. Depending on the structure of the variance, power to detect trends can be increased by altering the sampling design. For example, if the vast majority of the variance is spatial, power may be increased by adding more sampling sites. Conversely, if coherent temporal variation is large, no amount of sampling design manipulation will reduce the influence of this source of variation on the power to detect trends. In this case, power will increase only after sampling has continued for a longer period of time. Ephemeral temporal variation can only be estimated by sampling specific sites multiple times within a year. To decrease this component of variance, more sites may be re-sampled within the same sampling period. If trend variation is large, sampling sites every year instead of every fourth year may increase power to detect trends. Residual variation may be difficult to affect by manipulating sampling design; however, clear data collection protocols and quality control assurances in the data handling processes may help reduce the human-caused components of residual variation (Urquhart et al., 1998).

Statistical power is the probability of rejecting the null hypothesis when it is, in fact, false (i.e., detecting a trend when a trend is present). Several factors influence our ability to detect change over time, including sample size, the probability of a type-I error (α), the probability of a type-II error (β), trend magnitude, and variance. Type-I error (or "false change") refers to falsely detecting a trend when no trend is present. Type-II error (or "missed change") refers to wrongly concluding that no trend is present when, in fact, there is a trend. Power is equal to $1-\beta$. Common accepted values of α and β range from 0.01 to 0.2 (Irwin 2008). The Vegetation and Soil Monitoring Protocol (Perles et al. 2010) suggests that this monitoring program should ideally be able to detect a 20% change in key parameters over five or ten years (i.e., two or three plot revisits), with a power of 0.80 and an α of 0.1.

Random effects models have been used to partition variability in fish data (Osenberg et al. 1998, Wagner et al. 2007). However, to our knowledge, a components-of-variance approach has not been applied to forest vegetation data. The objective of this study was to perform power analyses to assess the ability of the ERMN Vegetation Monitoring Program to detect trends in 30 key measures of forest structure, function, or dynamics. At the forest monitoring plots, data are collected on numerous components of the forest stand. The sampling design may provide an adequate sample size for some measurements, but may not be adequate for others. If adequate power is not attained for some measures after the first cycle of sampling, adequate power may be achieved after several repetitions (Urquhart et al. 1998).

Methods

Although a brief overview of the vegetation and soil monitoring methods is provided here, a detailed rationale of the sampling design and methods, in addition to data collection Standard Operating Procedures, are provided in the Vegetation and Soil Monitoring Protocol (Perles et al. 2010). The protocol was based on the U.S. Forest Service (USFS) Forest Inventory and Analysis (FIA) program (USFS 2007) and the vegetation monitoring protocols of four other Inventory and Monitoring programs in the eastern United States (Sanders et al. 2006, Schmit et al. 2006, Comiskey et al. 2009, Tierney et al. 2009). Adopting widely used protocols facilitates comparisons of ERMN data with other NPS networks and regional data sets.

Sampling Design

Vegetation and soil are monitored at permanent plots. The decision to use permanent plots versus sampling new, randomly selected plots each year was made because the use of permanent plots has been shown to provide greater power to detect trends through time (Urquhart et al. 1998). For each park, a regular grid of potential plot locations was overlain on the park. Sampling locations were selected from the regular grid using a generalized random-tessellation stratified (GRTS) design (McDonald 2004, Stevens and Olsen 2004). The three main advantages to a GRTS design are: 1) the GRTS design is spatially balanced, wherein there is generally uniform dispersion of sampling sites over the area of interest; 2) the GRTS design allows for flexible sample size, such that sites can be added to or excluded from the sampling plan without compromising the integrity of the overall design; and 3) the GRTS method is a probabilistic sampling design, whereby sampling points are randomly chosen from among those in a systematic grid, eliminating site selection bias, and allowing inference to the entire sampling frame (Stevens and Olsen 2004).

Plots are sampled on a four-year simple panel design, in which one panel containing one-fourth of a park's total plots is sampled each year (Figure 2a). On the fifth year, the vegetation in the first panel of plots is re-sampled. An alternative design is a connected panel (Figure 2b) in which some plots are visited every year (common panel) in addition to the plots that are revisited once every fifth year. This connectivity can provide increased power to detect trends by allowing for the estimation of site-by-year variance earlier in the sampling design (Urquhart et al. 1998, Urquhart and Kincaid 1999). However, this design would incur increased cost and would expose plots to additional sampling impacts.

ERMN vegetation and soil sampling began in 2007. Between 2007 and 2011 there were 360 plots established in the eight parks (Table 1). This sample size was determined primarily by budgetary and logistical constraints such as length of growing season and availability of qualified crew members. The ERMN Vegetation Monitoring Program budget currently contains sufficient funds for one crew of three people over 15 weeks (the length of most university summer breaks). Based on the preliminary experiences of other NPS networks that had implemented vegetation monitoring programs, ERMN estimated that our crew could realistically sample between 300 and 400 plots over a four-year cycle. Thus, we divided a projected 350 total plots among the network's parks to ensure a minimum sample size for statistical inference in the smaller ERMN parks (n≥12), while allocating sufficient resources to the larger parks (n=102).

(a)

Panel	\multicolumn{12}{c}{Year}											
	1	2	3	4	5	6	7	8	9	10	11	12
1	X				X				X			
2		X				X				X		
3			X				X				X	
4				X				X				X

(b)

Panel	\multicolumn{12}{c}{Year}											
	1	2	3	4	5	6	7	8	9	10	11	12
1	X				X				X			
2		X				X				X		
3			X				X				X	
4				X				X				X
Common	X	X	X	X	X	X	X	X	X	X	X	X

Figure 2. Schematic for (a) simple panel and (b) connected panel designs.

Table 1. The number and type of monitoring plots sampled in ERMN parks from 2007–2011. New plots are in green, revisit plots are in blue and orange, and observer error revisits are in red. Acronyms for the parks are: Allegheny Portage Railroad National Historic Site (ALPO), Bluestone National Scenic River (BLUE), Delaware Water Gap National Recreation Area (DEWA), Fort Necessity National Battlefield (FONE), Friendship Hill National Historic Site (FRHI), Gauley River National Recreation Area (GARI), Johnstown Flood National Memorial (JOFL), and New River Gorge National River (NERI).

2007	NERI	DEWA	JOFL	ALPO	FONE	FRHI	GARI	BLUE	Total
New Plots for 2007	20	26	1	3	5	5	12	12	84
2008									
New Plots for 2008	29	26	3	6	5	5	9	9	92
Revisit of 2007 Plots	5	5					2	2	14
Observer Error Revisits		3							3
Total	34	34	3	6	5	5	11	11	109
2009									
New Plots for 2009	25	25	3	6	5	5	9	9	87
Revisit of 2007 Plots	5	5							10
Revisit of 2008 Plots	2	5							7
Observer Error Revisits		3							3
Total	32	38	3	6	5	5	9	9	107
2010									
New Plots for 2010	26	25	3	6	5	5	10	10	90
Revisit of 2007 Plots	5	5							10
Revisit of 2008 Plots	2	3							5
Observer Error Revisits		2						1	3
Total	33	35	3	6	5	5	10	11	108
2011									
Revisit of 2007 Plots	20	26	1	3	5	5	12	12	84
New Plots for 2011	2		2	3					7
Revisit of 2008 Plots	2	5							7
Observer Error Revisits		2						1	3
Total	24	33	3	6	5	5	13	12	101

To evaluate the costs and benefits of a connected panel design, we experimented with a preliminary connected panel design. A subset of plots from 2007 and 2008 were visited every year as part of the common panel (Table 1). During revisits, plots are sampled within two weeks of the original sampling date to minimize the effects of seasonal variation on the data. In addition, each year three plots from the panel were selected to be resampled as quality control measure. The three plots were resampled within a few weeks of the original sampling; however, crew members switched roles for the resampling, such that the original data recorder was responsible for taking measurements during the revisit. If possible, a different botanist sampled the quadrats during the revisits. Table 1 lists the number of new, revisited, and observer error plots that were sampled each year between 2007 and 2011.

Field Methods

At each plot, the ERMN monitors a suite of vegetation and soil variables. The plot design includes several embedded sampling units (Figure 3). Tree, stand, and site measurements are collected within fixed-area 15-m radius circular plots. Tree regeneration and shrub measurements are collected on four 2-m radius circular microplots embedded within each plot. Data on coarse woody debris are collected using line intersect sampling along six 15-m transects. Data on understory plant composition and the diversity of understory species are monitored using twelve 1-m² quadrats set along the six transects. A photograph of the plot is taken from the plot's southern edge to document change in vegetation structure through time. Three soil samples are collected from sampling frames located adjacent to the plot's northern edge. For complete description of data collection methods see Perles et al. (2010).

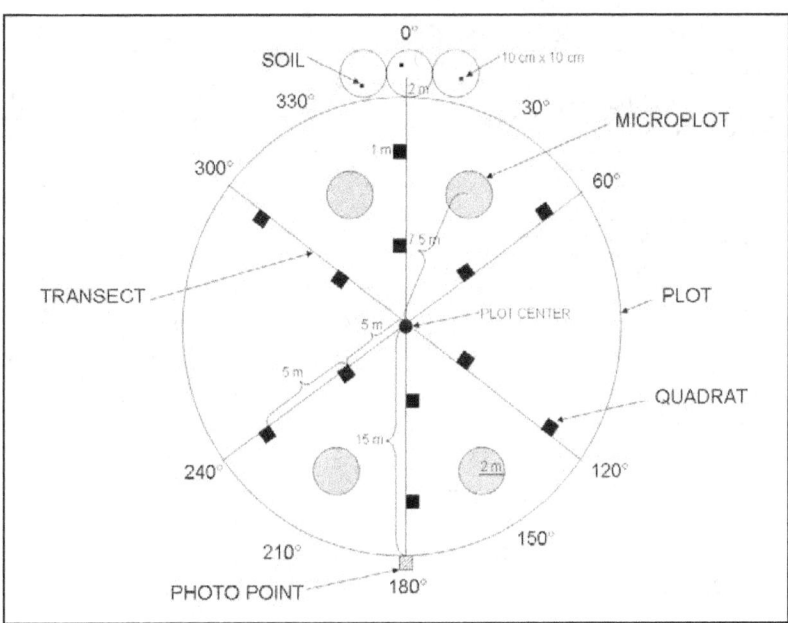

Figure 3. Plot design for Eastern Rivers and Mountains Network Vegetation and Soil Monitoring protocol.

Data Analysis

Thirty variables covering a wide range of forest metrics (Table 2) were included in this study. Either four or five years of data were used depending on the availability of the data at time of analysis. Some data from 2007 could not be included due to differences in data collection procedures during the first year of sampling. Some data from 2011 were not yet available at the time of analysis. All of the non-count variables were natural log transformed prior to statistical analysis. The count variables were not transformed.

Table 2. Thirty forest health variables selected for the evaluation of the sampling design's statistical power to detect temporal trends. Data are identified as Count Data and Non-count Data, see Statistical Analysis section.

Variable	Count Data	Non-count Data	Years of Data Used
Groundstory Diversity			
Total Quadrat Species Richness	X		2008-2011
Walk Around Species Richness	X		2008-2011
Total Groundstory Species Richness (Quad + Walk Around)	X		2008-2011
Floristic Quality Index		X	2008-2011
Number of Key Invasive Exotics Present	X		2007-2011
Proportion of Total Species Richness in Native Species		X	2007-2011
Proportion of Total Species Richness in Non-Native Species		X	2007-2011
Proportion of Total Species Richness in Invasive Species		X	2007-2011
Proportion of Total Cover in Native Species		X	2007-2011
Proportion of Total Cover in Non-Native Species		X	2007-2011
Proportion of Total Cover in Invasive Exotic Species		X	2008-2011
Total Cover of Invasive Exotic Species		X	2008-2011
Average Cover of Invasive Exotic Species		X	2008-2011
Total Cover of Rhizomatous Ferns		X	2007-2010
Browse Indicators			
Total Number of Individuals (all species)	X		2007-2011
Total Number of Individuals of Canada mayflower	X		2007-2011
Average Height of Tallest Jack-in-the-Pulpit[1]		X	2007-2010
Tree Regeneration and Shrubs			
Average Stocking Index		X	2007-2010
Total Seedling Species Richness	X		2007-2011
Total Sapling Basal Area		X	2007-2010
Total Sapling Density	X		2007-2011
Total Seedling Density	X		2007-2011
Total Number of Shrub Stems	X		2007-2011
Total Shrub Cover		X	2007-2010
Total Shrub Species Richness	X		2007-2011
Coarse Woody Debris			
Average CWD Volume		X	2007-2010
Trees			
Live Basal Area		X	2007-2010
Live Density	X		2007-2011
Snag Basal Area		X	2007-2010
Snag Density	X		2007-2011

[1] data were used only from plots that contained Jack-in-the-Pulpit in the 1-m2 quadrats.

Statistical Analysis

For the non-count data (Table 2), a linear mixed model was used to partition the total variance in 17 key forest metrics, similar to the approach suggested by Piepho and Ogutu (2002). The mixed model used for the analyses was:

$$(1) \qquad y_{ijk} = \mu + a_i + year_j(\lambda + t_i) + b_j + c_{ij} + e_{ijk}$$

where y_{ijk} is the forest metric from the kth sample for plot i in year j, and μ and λ are the fixed intercept and slope (fixed regional trend), respectively. The random effect a_i is a random effect for plot i, representing plot-to-plot (spatial) variability, independent and independently distributed (iid) as $N(\sigma_a^2)$; b_j is a random effect for the jth year (coherent temporal variability), iid as $N(0, \sigma_b^2)$; t_i is a random effect for the trend for plot i, iid as $N(0, \sigma_t^2)$; c_{ij} is the plot × year interaction (ephemeral temporal variability), iid as $N(0, \sigma_c^2)$; e_{ijk} is the unexplained error (residual error), independent as $N(0, \sigma_e^2)$. The year covariate (*year*) is the jth year minus the mean year used in the analysis. This standardization of year was performed to provide numerical stability. We estimated variance components using restricted maximum likelihood and considered all analyses significant at $P<0.05$.

For the count data, negative binomial mixed models were used to quantify temporal and spatial variability of the 13 variables (Table 2). Thus, we assume that $Y_{ijk} \sim NB(\mu_{ijk}, \kappa)$ where Y_{ijk} is the kth sample of each indicator at site i in year j, μ_{ijk} is the expected value for that sample, site and year, and κ is the scaling parameter of negative binomial distribution. We employ a log-link function such that, generally, the $\log_e$ of the expected value would be a linear function of the predictors:

$$(2) \qquad \eta_{ijk} = v + a_i + year_j(\lambda + t_i) + b_j + c_{ij}$$

where η_{ijk} is the $\log_e$ of the expected value of each metric from the kth sample at site i in year j, v is the fixed intercept, and λ is the fixed slope for temporal trends using year as the covariate (i.e., the predictor variable). The terms a_i (plot-to-plot effects), t_i (plot-specific trend effects), b_j (coherent temporal effects) and c_{ij} (ephemeral temporal effects) are all random effects as described above, independent and independently distributed (iid) as $N(0, \sigma_x^2)$; where (σ_x^2) is the unique variance parameter for each random effect. For each indicator variable separately, the year covariate was centered on its mean value in an attempt to improve model convergence. Therefore, $year_j$ represents a centered value of j.

All parameter estimation was conducted using the Random Effects module of AD Model Builder (ADMB), statistical programming software for fitting nonlinear models (http://www.admb-project.org/). More details on the variance-component framework and these estimation procedures can be found in Wagner et al. (2007) and Irwin et al. (2011).

Initially, data from all of the parks were used in the mixed models to estimate the components of variance. Ultimately, only data from DEWA were used in the models for three reasons: 1) to minimize the spatial variability, which was the largest proportion of the total variance; 2) to limit the number of potential plots in the simulation (described below) such that the simulations could be completed in a reasonable period of time (48–96 hours of continuous computing time); and 3) of the two large parks in the network (DEWA and NERI), only DEWA contained revisited plots from the common panel and observer error revisits necessary to calculate all the components of variance. The only exception was the coarse woody debris data set of xeric plots. For that data set, all xeric plots from NERI, GARI, and BLUE were used because the common panel plots were in xeric settings and two observer error revisits had been sampled in those parks.

We used a simulation approach to examine the statistical power to detect temporal trends in 17 non-count variables and four count variables using the variance components estimate from equations 1 and 2, respectively. Similar simulation approaches are discussed in Wagner et al. (2007) and (2009). For each simulation, 1,000 data sets were generated containing data on a particular forest metric for a population of potential plots in a park over 30 years. First, a true mean value for the forest metric was generated for each plot over the 30-year time period. Second, an average trend of pre-specified magnitude (e.g. an increase of 1% of the forest metric·year^{-1}) was incorporated into the data set (each site could deviate from this mean, with the deviation dependent on the magnitude of the trend variance component). Although we restricted our analysis to the investigation of linear trends, if a monotonic increase or decrease is present, then a linear trend will be present (Urquhart and Kincaid 1999). From these 1,000 data sets, a user-specified number of plots (ranging from three to 25) were then randomly sampled from the population of potential plots in a park (ranging from 60 to 500) each year. Plots were sampled either with a simple 4-year panel design in which a specified number of plots were sampled in each panel (ranging from three to 25), or with a connected 4-year panel design in which one fifth of the plots were sampled every year in the common panel. Data were analyzed for the presence of a trend over different sampling durations: from three up to 30 years. The models specified in equation 1 and 2 were used to test the null hypothesis that $\hat{\lambda}=0$ for non-count and count data, respectively, and the test statistic was calculated and compared with a critical value ($\alpha=0.05$). Because the data generated depict a situation in which we know the null hypothesis is false (i.e. a trend of pre-specified magnitude was incorporated into the data), power was estimated as the percentage of trials (out of 1,000) that rejected the null hypothesis.

We investigated the extent to which the following factors affected the ability to detect a trend:

- Using a simple panel versus a connected panel design
- Increasing the trend magnitude (λ ranged from 1 to 10% change in a forest metric·year-1)
- Varying sample size in relation to park size (ranging from 3 to 25 plots· year-1)
- Post-stratifying the plots into vegetation domains (xeric and mesic)
- Increasing the coherent temporal variation (from 0–10% of total variation)

For most of these scenarios, the variance component estimates for coarse woody debris volume from DEWA were used since this variable had moderate power. This was done because increases or decreases in power influenced by the factors outlined above would be more easily observed in a variable with moderate power compared to one with very high (e.g., 100%) power.

Results

Partitioning of Variance Using Mixed Models

For the non-count data, all models ran to convergence. The slope, total variance, and percent of total variance in different variance components are shown in Table 3. Slope provides an estimate of the yearly change occurring for each variable over the past 4 to 5 years. For most variables, the vast majority of the total variance was spatial. Total variance for total cover of rhizomatous ferns, average cover of invasive exotic species, and total cover of invasive exotic species was much higher than for the other variables.

For the count data, the estimation procedure ran to completion for all of the variables except for total number of Canada mayflower. However, convergence warnings were produced for the majority of the variables (Table 3), suggesting that the model was not generating reliable estimates for all parameters. Inspection of the resulting parameter estimates suggested that the model was likely having trouble estimating several of the temporal variance parameters (Table 3), likely due to the relatively short (4 or 5 years) nature of the time series and because incorporating spatial effects into the model appeared to allow for close approximation of the observed data. The high percent of the total variance in residual variation in these cases does not necessarily refer to observer error while collecting field measurement. It refers to all of the remaining unexplained variation. It is likely that some of this variation was temporal variation that could not be estimated separately by the model. Power simulations were run only for the four count variables which did not produce convergence warnings during model estimation (Table 3).

Power to Detect Trends in Forest Health Variables

Overall, the simulations indicate that the current sampling design for the ERMN Forest and Soil Monitoring Program will likely yield greater than 80% power to detect a 1% trend $\cdot$ year^{-1} in most key variables within two to three sampling cycles (10–15 years, Table 4) at the two largest ERMN parks. Power curves for these simulations are shown in Appendix A. For some variables, such as coarse woody debris volume, average stocking index, total shrub cover, total cover of invasive species, and average cover of invasive species, the sampling design never attains 80% power to detect a 1% trend $\cdot$ year^{-1} even after 30 years. The total variance for these variables was larger (>1) than for the other non-count variables. For Jack-in-the-pulpit height and cover of rhizomatous ferns, power to detect a 1% trend $\cdot$ year^{-1} exceeded 80% only after 15–20 years. Power curves for the count variables indicate that the sampling design will likely yield greater than 80% power to detect a 5% trend $\cdot$ year^{-1} within one to two sampling cycles (5–10 years), but will not yield greater than 80% power to detect a 1% trend $\cdot$ year^{-1} until after three sampling cycles (>15 years) for three of the four variables (Appendix A, Table 4). The sampling design is likely overly intensive for detecting a 5% trend $\cdot$ year^{-1} in the two largest parks for nearly all of the key variables, since the simulations showed nearly 100% power for all variables after 12 years (Table 4).

Table 3. Percent of total variance in each of five variance components, total variance and slope estimated by mixed models for 30 forest health variables.

Non-count Variables	Spatial	Coherent Temporal	Ephemeral Temporal	Trend	Residual	Total Variance	Slope	Slope Standard Error
Average Height of Tallest Jack-in-the-Pulpit	73.82%	3.11%	3.43%	13.76%	5.88%	0.1645	0.1243	0.0558
Proportion of Total Species Richness in Native Species	87.48%	2.19%	4.83%	0.00%	5.51%	0.0119	0.0044	0.0068
Proportion of Total Cover in Non-Native Species	91.11%	0.64%	3.00%	5.19%	0.05%	0.0366	0.0051	0.0081
Proportion of Total Cover in Native Species	91.16%	0.00%	3.88%	1.11%	3.85%	0.0262	0.0028	0.0060
Floristic Quality Index	91.89%	1.07%	0.24%	0.00%	6.80%	0.0810	0.0018	0.0167
Coarse Woody Debris Volume	93.18%	0.00%	1.02%	4.74%	1.05%	1.6528	0.0703	0.0616
Total Sapling Basal Area	94.34%	0.00%	0.00%	5.24%	0.42%	0.0135	-0.0031	0.0044
Proportion of Total Species Richness in Nonnative Species	95.43%	0.14%	3.28%	0.98%	0.17%	0.0175	0.0040	0.0045
Total Shrub Cover	95.63%	1.51%	2.14%	0.13%	0.58%	1.4449	0.1501	0.0853
Average Stocking Index	95.64%	0.00%	0.63%	2.82%	0.91%	1.7336	0.0619	0.0527
Snag Basal Area	96.58%	0.29%	1.25%	1.86%	0.01%	0.4706	0.0499	0.0329
Total Cover of Rhizomatous Ferns	97.42%	1.41%	0.06%	0.00%	1.11%	4.7291	-0.0312	0.1236
Average Cover of Invasive Exotic Species	98.21%	0.00%	0.53%	0.00%	1.27%	3.0173	-0.1229	0.0463
Total Cover of Invasive Exotic Species	98.87%	0.00%	0.43%	0.00%	0.71%	7.9293	-0.1223	0.0647
Proportion of Total Cover in Invasive Species	99.09%	0.00%	0.10%	0.79%	0.02%	0.0370	0.0013	0.0031
Proportion of Total Species Richness in Invasive Species	99.23%	0.00%	0.18%	0.00%	0.59%	0.0171	0.0003	0.0022
Live Tree Basal Area	99.89%	0.00%	0.09%	0.02%	0.00%	0.7860	0.0214	0.0091
Count Variables [1]								
Total Shrub Species Richness	46.46%	0.00%	0.00%	0.00%	53.54%	0.3798	0.1046	--
Total Seedling Species Richness	51.76%	0.00%	0.00%	0.00%	48.24%	0.3047	0.1001	--
Number of Key Invasive Exotic Species Present	65.19%	0.00%	0.00%	0.00%	34.81%	3.2671	0.0771	--
Snag Density	65.94%	0.00%	0.00%	0.00%	34.06%	1.5185	0.0418	--
Total Sapling Density	66.54%	0.00%	0.00%	0.00%	33.46%	3.1686	-0.0079	--
Walk Around Species Richness	73.71%	0.00%	0.00%	0.00%	26.29%	0.2432	-0.0947	0.0259
Total Number of Individuals of Browse Indicators	81.81%	0.00%	0.00%	0.00%	18.19%	11.5714	0.0080	--
Total Quadrat Species Richness	85.81%	0.00%	0.00%	0.00%	14.19%	0.2928	0.0058	--
Total Groundstory Species Richness	88.39%	0.00%	0.00%	0.00%	11.61%	0.2116	-0.0270	--
Live Tree Density	89.01%	0.00%	0.00%	0.00%	10.99%	0.4389	0.0074	0.0118
Total Seedling Density	92.46%	1.71%	0.77%	2.21%	2.86%	1.8934	0.1705	0.0648
Total Number Shrub Stems	94.75%	0.79%	0.11%	0.20%	4.15%	3.5003	0.0754	0.0578

[1] variables in italics produced convergence warnings during the model estimation, and the model was unable to estimate slope standard deviation for these variables.

Table 4. Power of sampling design to detect trends in key forest health variables after 12 years.

Non-count Variables	Power to detect 1% · year⁻¹ trend after 12 years	Power to detect 5% · year⁻¹ trend after 12 years
Coarse Woody Debris Volume	57.6%	100.0%
Total Cover of Invasive Exotic Species	60.5%	95.5%
Total Cover of Rhizomatous Ferns	63.4%	99.2%
Total Shrub Cover	67.7%	100.0%
Average Cover of Invasive Exotic Species	69.3%	100.0%
Average Stocking Index	71.8%	100.0%
Average Height of Tallest Jack-in-the-Pulpit	73.7%	100.0%
Snag Basal Area	85.5%	100.0%
Proportion of Total Species Richness in Native Species	87.4%	100.0%
Proportion of Total Cover in Non-Native Species	100.0%	100.0%
Proportion of Total Cover in Native Species	100.0%	100.0%
Floristic Quality Index	100.0%	100.0%
Total Sapling Basal Area	100.0%	100.0%
Proportion of Total Species Richness in Nonnative Species	100.0%	100.0%
Proportion of Total Cover in Invasive Species	100.0%	100.0%
Proportion of Total Species Richness in Invasive Species	100.0%	100.0%
Live Tree Basal Area	100.0%	100.0%
Count Variables		
Walk Around Species Richness	53.5%	100.0%
Live Tree Density	56.1%	100.0%
Total Seedling Density	54.6%	95.3%
Total Number Shrub Stems	65.5%	80.3%

In general, variables that measure the proportion of the total species richness or total cover yielded much higher power than variables that measure absolute total cover or average cover. We propose that this is explained by the fact that using the proportion reduces the variability in cover measurements caused by yearly weather patterns (e.g., temperature and precipitation) and different observers.

Effect of Sampling Design and Trend Magnitude

The simple panel and connected panel designs had similar power estimates for detecting temporal trends (Figure 4). Within the first five years, the connected panel design initially exhibited slightly higher power than the simple panel design, but this advantage was not retained in subsequent years. This pattern is similar regardless of the magnitude of trend (1–10% · year⁻¹) that is being detected. Power curves in Figure 4 illustrate that increasing the magnitude of the trend increases the power to detect that trend. Given these results, the added cost of implementing the connected panel is not justified, especially considering the potential for annual sampling to impact the vegetation (e.g. trampling). In addition, for some key field measurements, such as tree diameter-at-breast-height (DBH), the average annual change (0.38 cm for DBH) is nearly equivalent to the average error in field measurement (0.27 cm for DBH). For measurements such as DBH, yearly sampling would add unnecessary "noise" to the data since observer error is nearly equal to the average annual change.

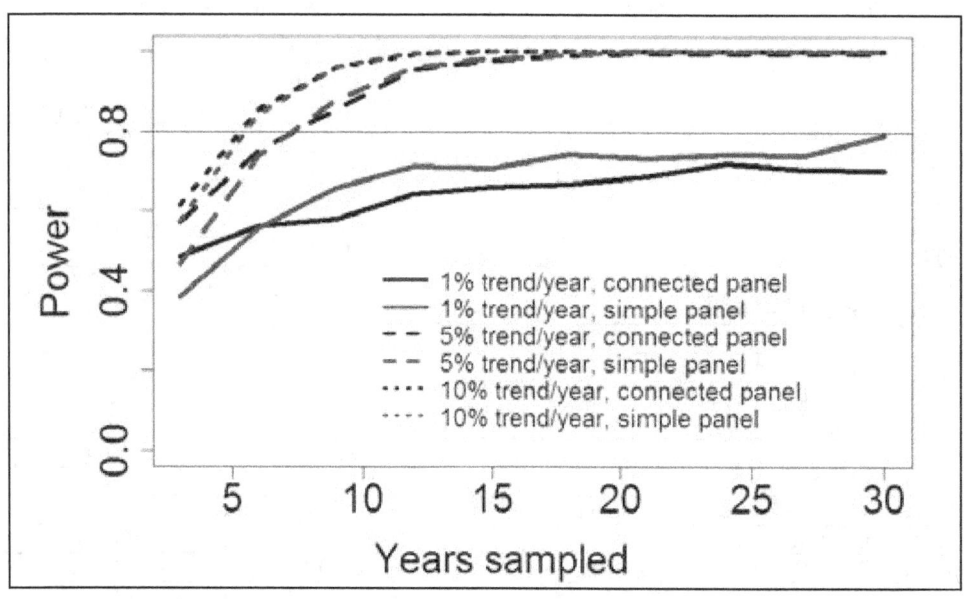

Figure 4. Power to detect trends in coarse woody debris volume using two sampling designs.

Effect of Sample Size

The sampling effort varies among ERMN parks in relation to park size (Table 1), ranging approximately from 3–25 plots · park[-1] · year[-1]. Using variance components estimated from coarse woody debris data in DEWA only, simulations were run with sample sizes similar to those in four parks (i.e., DEWA with 25 plots · year[-1], BLUE with 10 plots · year[-1], FONE with 5 plots · year[-1], and JOFL with 3 plots · year[-1]). Simulations indicate that even at the smallest parks, the current sampling design is adequate to detect a 5% trend · year[-1] in coarse woody debris volume (Figure 5) and 1% trend · year[-1] in live tree basal area (Figure 6) within three sampling cycles. Power curves in Figures 5, 6, and 7 indicate that the sample size could be reduced by more than half and retain a similar level of power. These results could be interpreted to indicate that the sampling design is overly intense, and that a smaller number of plots could detect trends at an acceptable level for less time and cost investment. However, the larger parks contain diverse vegetation which could be analyzed separately since different trends may be occurring in different vegetation types (see Effect of Post-Stratification into Vegetation Domains below).

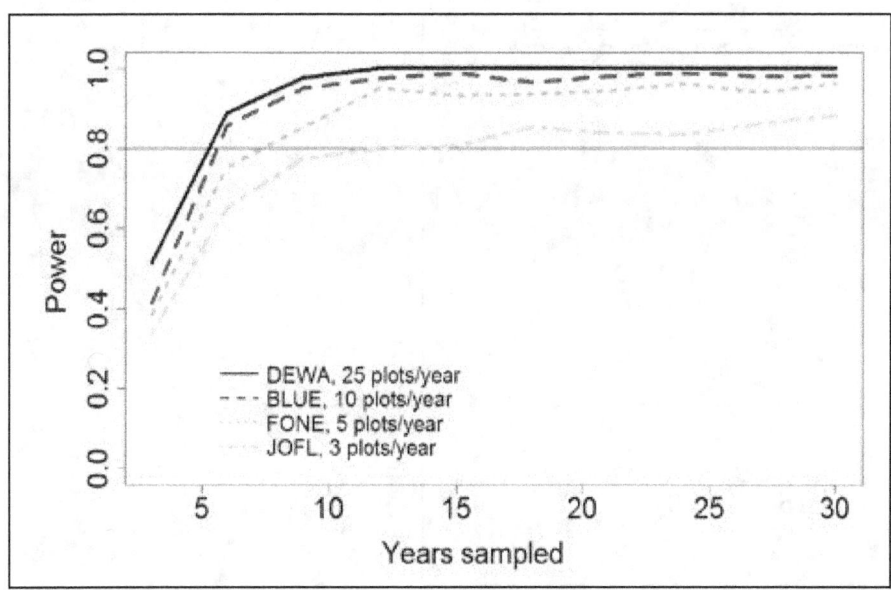

Figure 5. Power to detect a 5% trend · year^{-1} in coarse woody debris volume as simulated using different sample sizes for different parks.

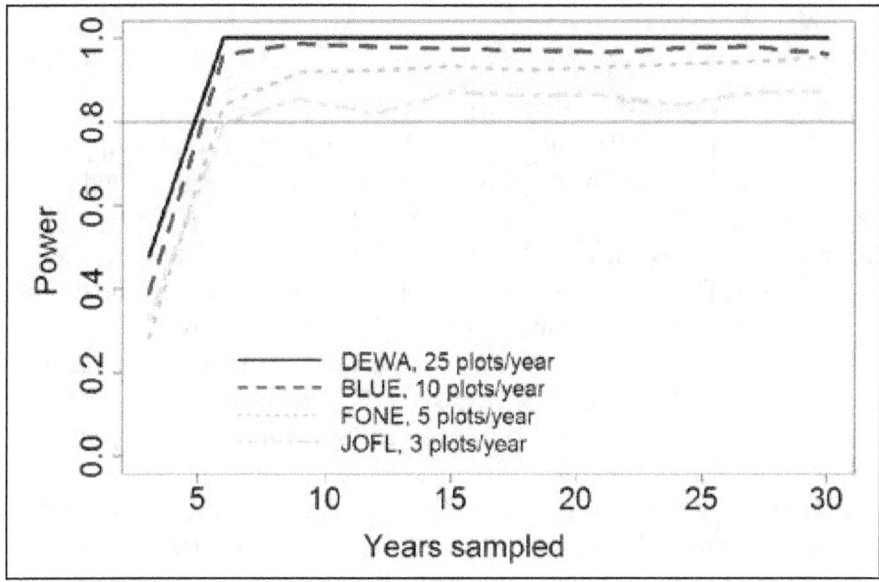

Figure 6. Power to detect 1% trend · year^{-1} in live tree basal area as simulated using different sample sizes for different parks.

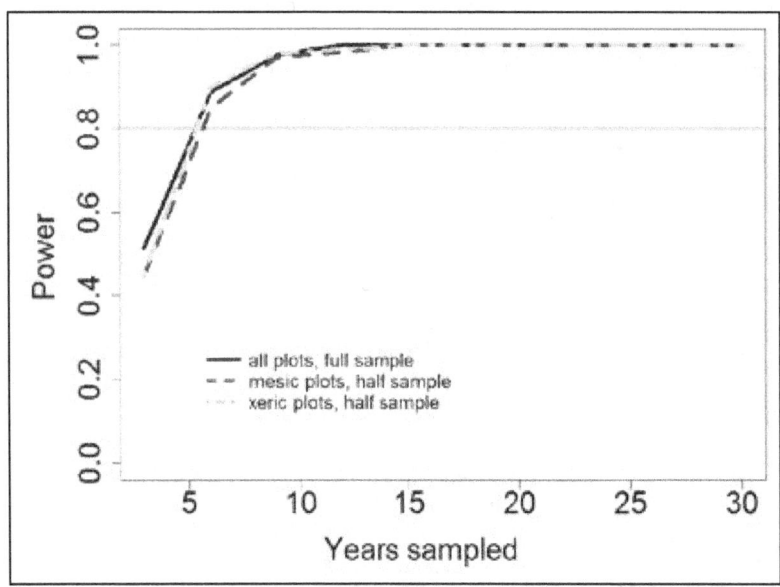

Figure 7. Power to detect 5% trend · year^{-1} in coarse woody debris volume using the variance components from all DEWA plots and simulating the full sample (25 plots · year^{-1}), the variance components from only mesic DEWA plots and simulating half the sample (13 plots · year^{-1}), and the variance components from only xeric plots in NERI, GARI, and BLUE and simulating half the sample (13 plots · year^{-1}).

Effect of Post-stratification into Vegetation Domains

In the larger ERMN parks (DEWA, NERI, GARI, and BLUE), the forests found on the upper slopes and ridgetops are very different than the forests growing on the lower slopes and valley bottoms. Xeric forests on higher topographic positions are dominated by oaks (*Quercus* spp.) and hickories (*Carya* spp.), often with ericaceous shrubs (e.g., blueberries, mountain laurel) in the understory. In the West Virginia parks, forests in lower topographic positions are often lush mixed mesophytic vegetation dominated by sugar maple (*Acer saccharum*), yellow buckeye (*Aesculus flava*), and American basswood (*Tilia americana*), with a wide diversity of herbaceous and graminoid plants in the understory. In DEWA, mesic forests are highly variable, due to the varied land use history in the river valley. It is possible that different trends in the key variables are occurring in the different forest types. Simulations using data from all four large parks indicate that power remains similar when plots are post-stratified by vegetation type, despite the corresponding reduction in sample size by half (Figure 7). For these simulations, the full sample (25 plots · year^{-1}) used the variance components calculated from all DEWA plots, the mesic simulations used variance components from only mesic DEWA plots and simulated half the sample (13 plots · year^{-1}), and the xeric simulation used variance components from only xeric plots in NERI, GARI, and BLUE and simulated half the sample (13 plots · year^{-1}).

Effect of Coherent Temporal Variation

For many of the key variables, the coherent temporal variation was estimated to be zero or very small (Table 3). The true value is likely greater than zero, however, we were unable to find any published values for coherent temporal variation in forest monitoring data. Therefore, we ran several simulations increasing the proportion of the total variance allocated to coherent temporal variation (Figure 8). The power to detect a 1% trend $\cdot$ year^{-1} was unaffected by the amount of coherent temporal variation. However, the power to detect a 5% trend $\cdot$ year^{-1} decreases with increasing coherent temporal variation. If the true value of coherent temporal variation is larger than the small values used in the simulations for many of the key variables, then actual power will be lower than reported in Table 4 and Appendix A.

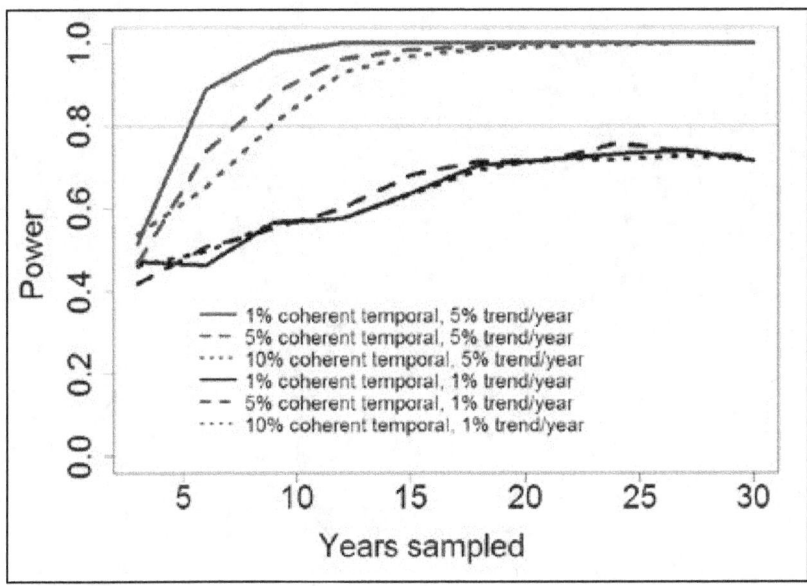

Figure 8. Power to detect 1% and 5% trend $\cdot$ year^{-1} in coarse woody debris volume with coherent temporal variance set a 1%, 5%, and 10% of the total variance.

Discussion

The simulations described herein provide an initial evaluation of the ERMN Forest and Soil Monitoring Program's statistical power to detect temporal trends. The program's sampling design is likely overly intensive for detecting a 5% trend · year^{-1} for all of the variables, is appropriate for detecting a 1% trend · year^{-1} in most variables, and is insufficient for detecting a 1% trend · year^{-1} for a few variables. However, these power estimates are "best case scenarios" since the estimates of coherent temporal variation and estimates of trend variation were likely underestimated based on only 4–5 years' of data. If the true value of coherent temporal variation is larger than the values used in the simulations, then actual power will be lower than reported here. Although the power curves reported here are potentially overly-optimistic, they suggest that the current sampling design is meeting the program's objectives.

Another important caveat is that most power simulations presented here are based on variance components calculated from data collected only in DEWA, primarily because the sampling design employed in DEWA provided the kinds of data necessary to calculate all of the components of variance. From a broad perspective (i.e., comparing ERMN forests to forests nationwide), DEWA forests are relatively similar to forests in the other ERMN parks; however, there are important differences among park forests that are influenced by geology, topography, land use history, distribution of forest pests, etc. These park-specific differences may influence the power of the sampling design in ways not captured by this analysis.

The total variance appeared more influential in determining power than the structure of the variance components. Similarly, Stow et al. (1998) found total variance to be one of the primary factors affecting the ability to detect trends. Variables that measure the proportion of a total (i.e., species richness or percent cover) yielded much higher power than variables that measure absolute or average values since using the proportion reduces the variability in cover measurements caused by yearly weather patterns and different observers.

There are sufficient samples in the larger ERMN parks to post-stratify plots by vegetation domains and retain adequate power. In the smaller parks, the small sample sizes currently employed are sufficient to detect small trends (1% · year^{-1}) in some important variables (i.e., live tree basal area). However, for some variables (e.g., coarse woody debris volume), only larger trends (5% · year^{-1}) will be detectable. Also, the connected panel design does not provide sufficient additional power over the simple panel design to justify the additional sampling cost. Similarly, Urquhart et al. (1993) found that connected panel design had the greatest benefit to trend detection within the first four years of sampling with negligible benefit after eight years.

The negative bionomial mixed models had convergence issues and thus were not able to estimate components of variance for most variables. The log-normal distribution models estimated some of the temporal components as zero or very small. These results are influenced by the short duration of time series data used to estimate parameters in these models. This inability to estimate some variance components could also be due to actual small magnitudes of specific variance components occurring for some forest indicators. The simulations could be conducted again in 2015 after all plots have been sampled twice. A larger data set spanning more years will provide improved estimates of components variance and power.

Literature Cited

Comiskey, J. A., J. P. Schmit, and G. Tierney. 2009. Mid-Atlantic Network forest vegetation monitoring protocol. Natural Resource Report NPS/MIDN/NRR—2009/119. National Park Service, Fort Collins, CO.

Fairweather, P.G. 1991. Statistical power and design requirements for environmental monitoring. Australian Journal of Marine and Freshwater Research 42:555–567.

Fancy, S. G., J. E. Gross, and S. L. Carter. 2009. Monitoring the condition of natural resources in US National Parks. Environmental Monitoring and Assessment 151:161–174.

Hatch, S. A. 1003. Statistical power for detecting trends with applications to seabird monitoring. Biological Conservation. 111:317–329.

Irwin, R. J. 2008. Part B Lite QA/QC Review Checklist for Aquatic Vital Signs Monitoring Protocols and SOPs. National Park Service. Water Resources Division. Fort Collins, CO. Distributed on the Internet only. (http://www.nature.nps.gov/water/VitalSigns_index/VitalSignsdocuments.cfm/).

Irwin, B. J., T. Wagner, M. V. Kepler, W. Liu, J. R. Bence, D. B. Hayes, and N. Lester. 2011. Spatial and temporal components of variation in Great Lake percid populations: implications for conservation and management. Great Lakes Fish and Wildlife Restoration Act, Project Completion Report.

Kincaid, T. M., D. P. Larsen, and N. S. Urquhart. 2004. The structure of variation and its influences on the estimation of status: indicators of condition of lakes in the northeast. U.S.A. Environmental Monitoring and Assessment. 98:1–21.

Larsen, D. P., T. M. Kincaid, S. E. Jacobs, and N. S. Urquhart. 2001. Designs for evaluating local and regional scale trends. Bioscience 51:1069–1078.

McDonald, T. L. 2004. GRTS for the Average Joe: A GRTS Sampler for Windows. (http://www.west-inc.com/biometrics_reports.php).

Marshall, M. R., and N. B. Piekielek. 2007. Eastern Rivers and Mountains Network Ecological Monitoring Plan. Natural Resource Report NPS/ERMN/NRR—2007/017. National Park Service. Fort Collins, CO.

Osenberg, C. W., E. E. Werner, G. G. Mittelback, and D. J. Hall. 1998. Growth patterns in bluegill (*Lepomis macrochirus*) and pumpkinseed (*L. gibbosus*) sunfish environmental variation and the importance of ontogenetic niche shifts. Canadian Journal of Fisheries and Aquatic Science. 45:17–26.

Perles, S., J. Finley, and M. Marshall. 2010. Vegetation and soil monitoring protocol for the Eastern Rivers and Mountains Network, Version 2. Natural Resource Report NPS/ERMN/NRR—2010/183. National Park Service. Fort Collins, CO.

Peterman, R .M. 1990. Statistical power analysis can improve fisheries research and management. Canadian Journal of Fisheries and Aquatic Sciences. 47:2–15.

Piepho, H.-P., and J. O. Ogutu. 2002. A simple mixed model for trend analysis in wildlife populations. Journal of Agricultural Biological and Environmental Statistics. 7:350–360.

Sanders, S., S. E. Johnson, and D. M. Waller. 2006. General vegetation monitoring protocol for the Great Lakes Network, Version 1.0. National Park Service, Great Lakes Network, Ashland, WI.

Schmit, J. P., D. C. Chojnacky, and M. Milton. 2006. Forest Monitoring Protocol, Version 1.0. National Park Service. National Capital Region Network. Washington, DC.

Stevens, D. L., and A. N. Olsen. 2004. Spatially balanced sampling of natural resources. Journal of American Statistical Association 99(465):262–278.

Stow, C. A., S. R. Carpenter, K. E. Weber, and T. M. Frost. 1998. Long-term environmental monitoring: some perspective from lakes. Ecological Applications. 8:269–276.

Tierney, G., B. Mitchell, K. Miller, J. Comiskey, A. Kozlowski, and D. Faber-Langendoen. 2009. Long-term forest monitoring protocol: Northeast Temperate Network. Natural Resource Report NPS/NETN/NRR—2009/117. National Park Service, Fort Collins, CO.

Urquhart, N. S., W. S. Overton, and D. S. Birkes. 1993. Comparing sampling designs for monitoring ecological status and trends: impact of temporal patterns. *Statistics for the Environment*, V. Barnett and K.F. Turkman, eds. John Wiley and Sons Ltd.

Urquhart, N. S., S. G. Paulsen, and D. P. Larsen. 1998. Monitoring for policy-relevant regional trends over time. Ecological Applications. 8:246–257.

Urquhart, N. S., and T. M. Kincaid. 1999. Designs for detecting trend from repeated surveys of ecological resources. Journal of Agricultural, Biological, and Environmental Statistics 4(4):404–414.

United States Forest Service (USFS). 2007. Forest Inventory and Analysis National Core Field Guide. Version 4.0. United States Forest Service.

Wagner, T., J. R. Bence, M. T. Gremigan, D. B. Hayes, and M. J. Wilberg. 2007. Regional trends in fish mean length at age: components of variance and the statistical power to detect trends. Canadian Journal of Fisheries and Aquatic Science. 64:968–978.

Wagner, T., C. S. Vandergoot, and J. Tyson. 2009. Evaluating the power to detect temporal trends in fishery-independent surveys: a case study based on gillnets set in the Ohio waters of Lake Erie for walleye. North American Journal of Fisheries Management. 29:805–816.

Appendix A. Power to detect trends in key forest health variables.

Using estimated components of variance modeled from monitoring plot data collected in DEWA, we used a simulation approach to examine the statistical power to detect 1% or 5% trend $\cdot$ year^{-1} in 17 non-count variables and 4 count variables. The simulation used a sampling design similar to that employed in DEWA and NERI, the two largest network parks. The power curves generated from these simulations are shown below.

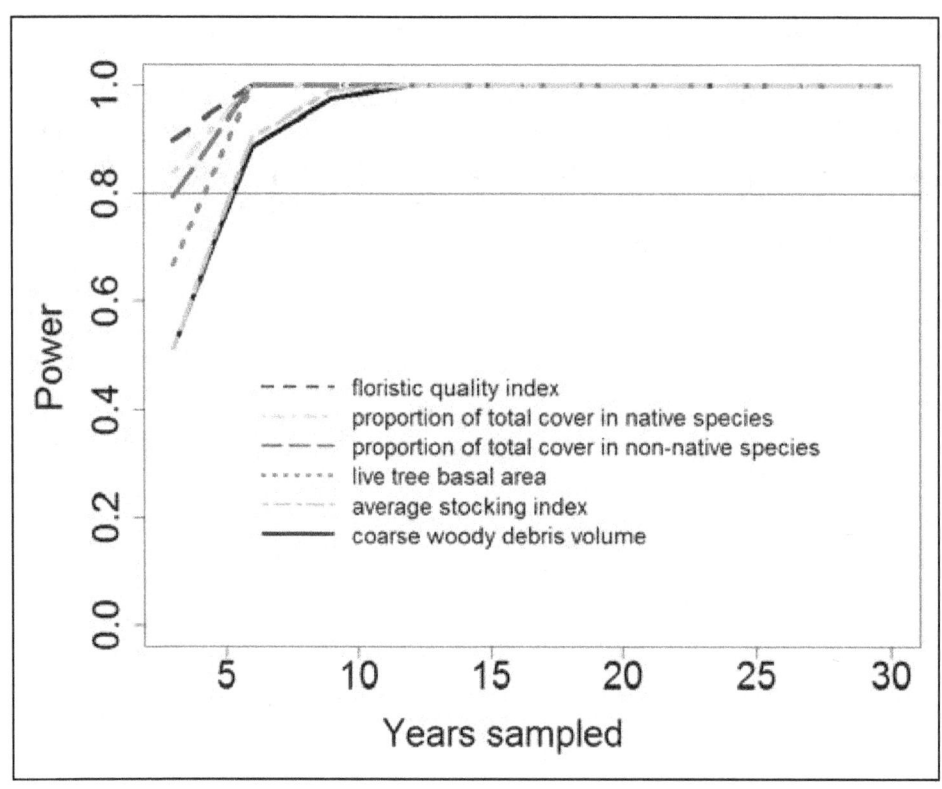

Figure A1. Power to detect a 5% trend · year^{-1} in 6 forest health variables.

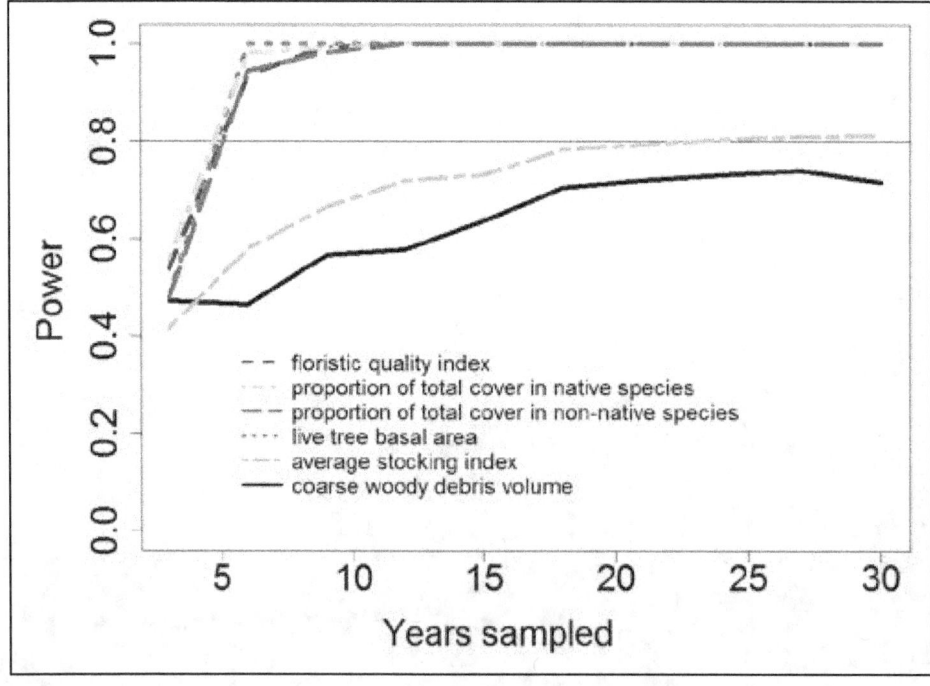

Figure A2. Power to detect a 1% trend · year-1 in 6 forest health variables.

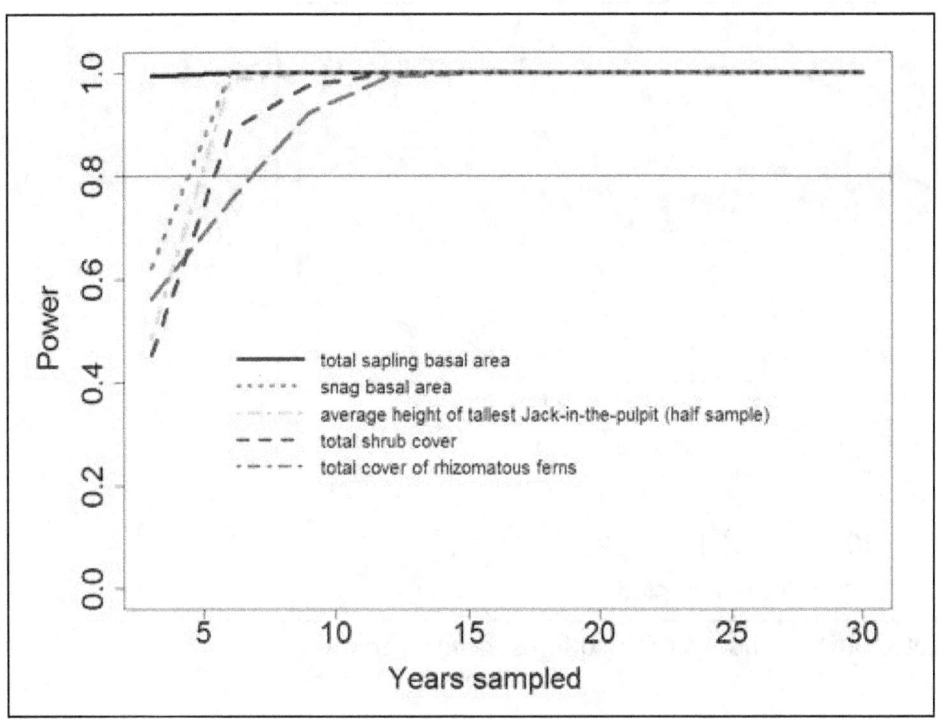

Figure A3. Power to detect a 5% trend · year^{-1} in 5 forest health variables.

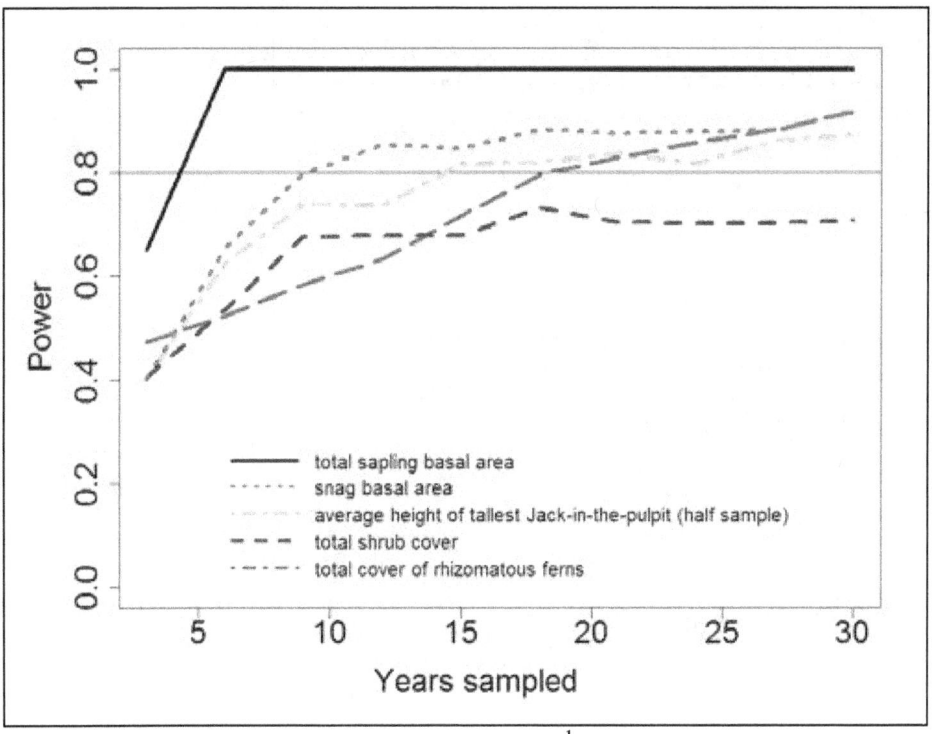

Figure A4. Power to detect a 1% trend · year^{-1} in 5 forest health variables.

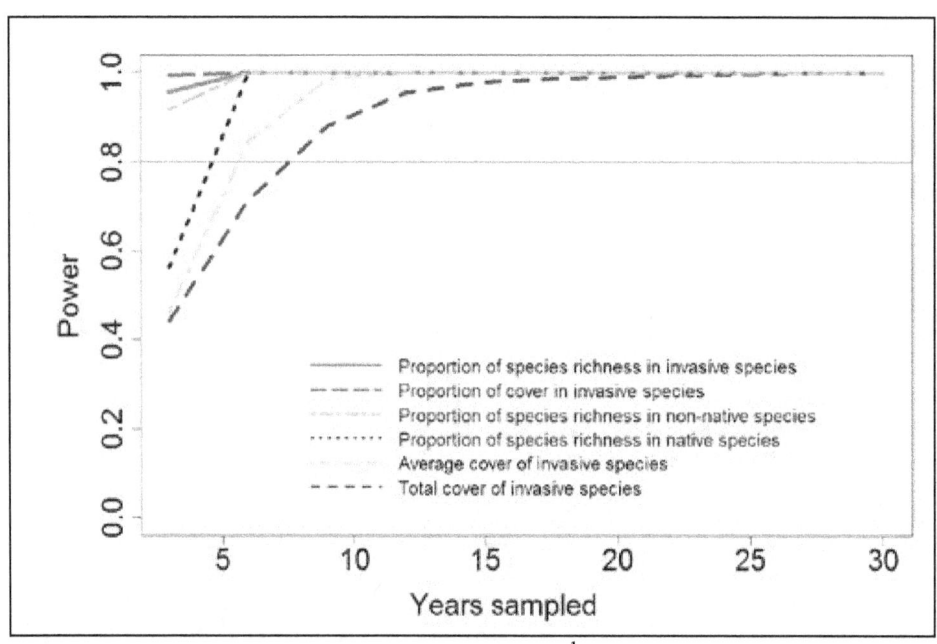

Figure A5. Power to detect a 5% trend · year^{-1} in 6 forest health variables.

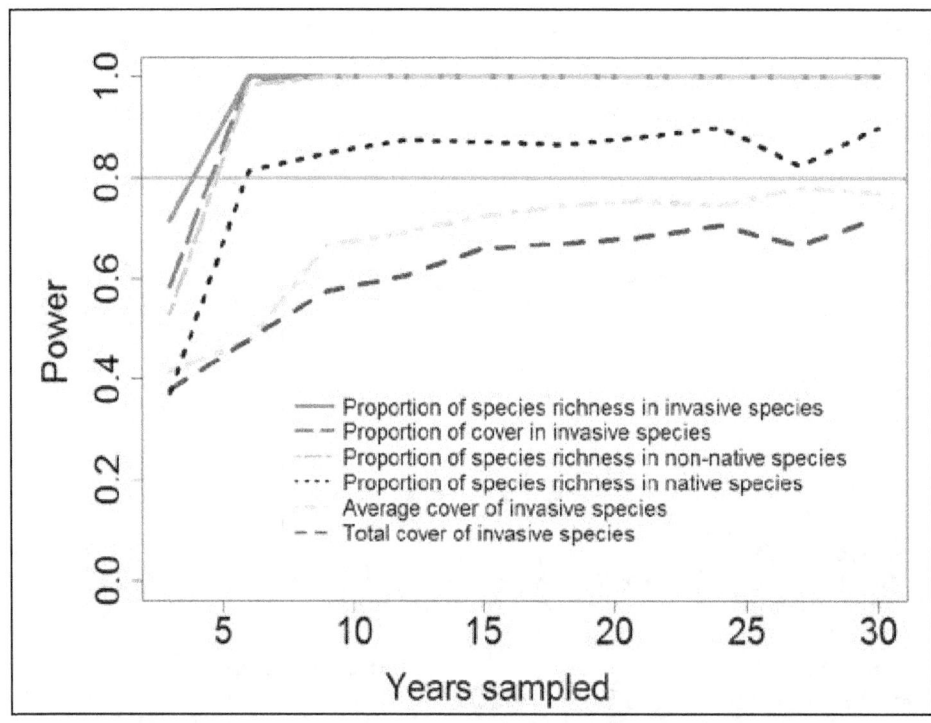

Figure A6. Power to detect a 1% trend · year^{-1} in 6 forest health variables.

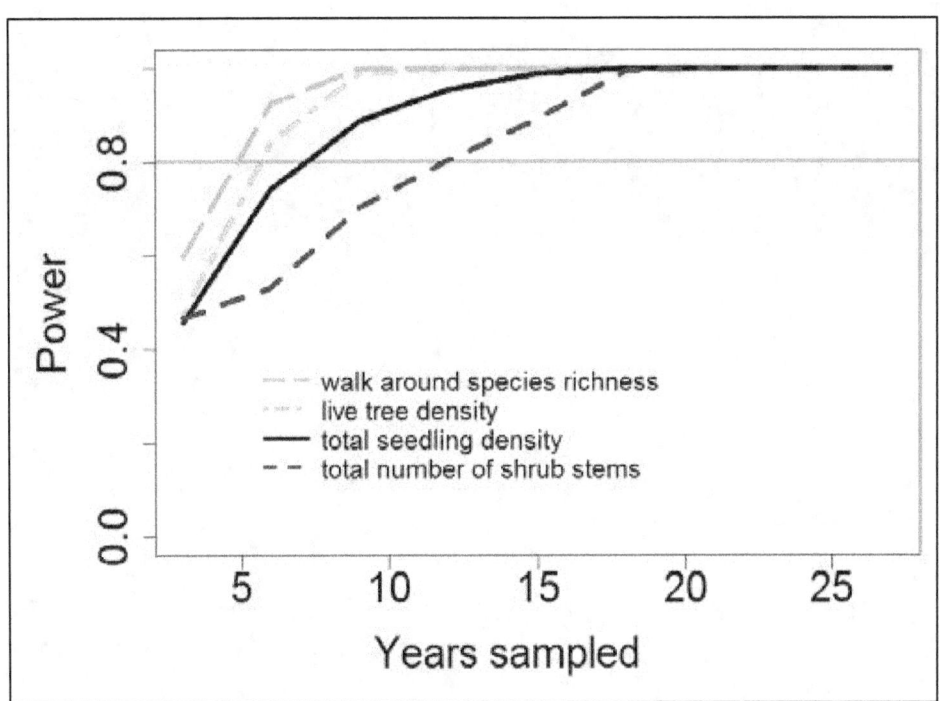

Figure A7. Power to detect a 5% trend · year^{-1} in four forest health count variables.

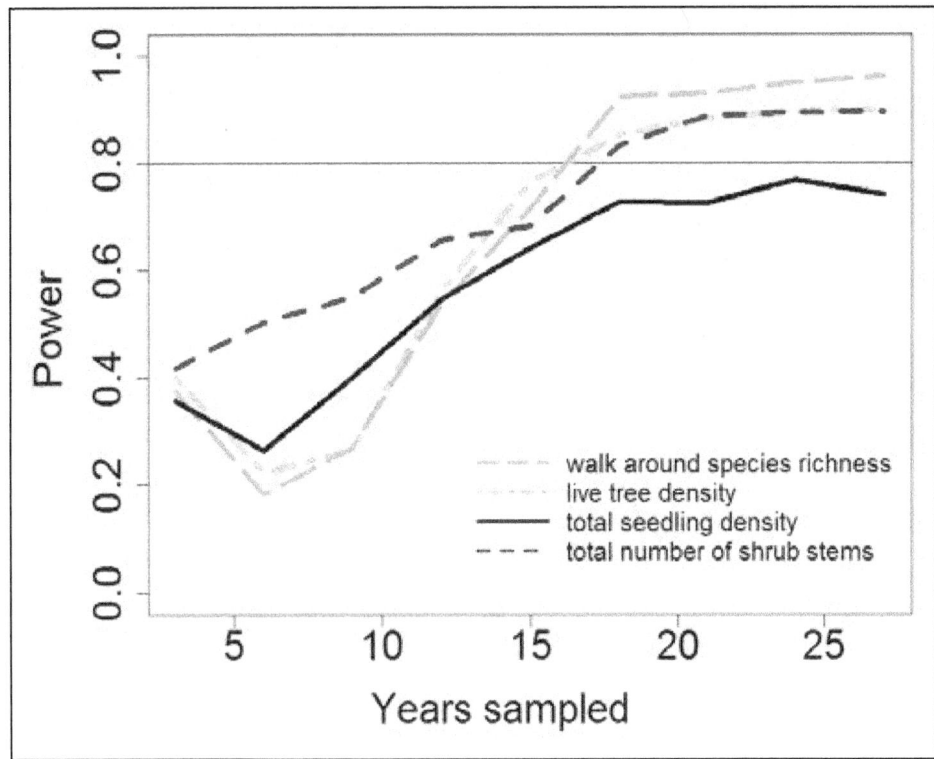

Figure A8. Power to detect a 1% trend · year^{-1} in four forest health count variables.

NPS 962/117418, October 2012